Christmas Poems

A Collection of Christmas card Christmas poems

By Erika Woo

ISBN 978-1-387-45827-1

Hello!

This is a collection of Christmas poems that I have written throughout the years. Since 2005, I have sent out a poem with my family's Christmas card; I have compiled them all here. That is, as much as I could find.... There are a few years that I am either missing the poem for or I didn't write one.

Each poem is printed exactly as it was sent out, fonts, text size etc. and I will admit, some of the formatting is awkward. I've also added the year if it wasn't in the original text. In addition to the yearly poems, I have added a few more that never made the cut and some annotations to each poem. By annotations, I mean short silly statements about my poetic abilities.

Thank you for reading my poems throughout the years, I hope you enjoyed reading them as much as I did writing.

Merry Christmas,
Erika

Table of Contents

The Good News Of Great Joy That Will Be For All The People

By Erika Woo 2022

And shepherds out in the fields at night
Did hear the good news first
From angel armies up on high
The Savior come for the cursed

Then wise men from the east did follow
The star up in the sky
Brought gifts of frankincense, gold, and myrrh
For the priestly king who'd die

Shepherds and wise men though different of walk
All came so humbly poised
Once met the baby in his crib
And they were overjoyed

So too I learn of Christ's manger bed
Still afraid to count this world as loss
I fight my sin myself but fail
And come joyfully to the cross

This year I had a pretty bad writer's block. I think it's because as I was compiling this book and reading through all my poems, I was wondering how I could top some of these and/or write about something I haven't yet.

So I did what anyone with writer's block would do: I read all of the poems by Stephen Crane I could find online until I was inspired.

I hope this poem conveys the humility, the hope and most importantly the joy that the good news of Christmas brings for everyone.

My office isn't a cubicle but I feel boxed in
Cardboard cut-outs of a childhood dream melt in the rain
And my umbrella breaks, letting the sideways wind attack
I shield myself for the blow that'll flatten me Stanley-style

The schedule slips and sloshes around on a whim
My brain juices sour, pickling my train of thought
The conductor pulls the last thread so a rug unravels
And I'm left on shiny hardwood floors with fluffy Hello Kitty socks

Advent advances quickly and I'm swept up in the whirl
Routine reels in response to spontaneity's range of motion
Surprise showers my face revealing panicked eyebrow hairs
If only I had a split-pea soup second to compose a prayer

As I panic and fuss, surround me with love's long comforter arms
Blanket waves of abundant peace on my eyelids, a whale-calm call
Remind me that you are here, present, unbowed and unwrapped
God's forever-promise fulfilled, Emmanuel, a Savior at long last

By Erika Woo, 2021

Yes, I understand, this poem can be confusing. It's as if I've thrown a bunch of images up in the air and they blend together and fall to the ground.

Simply put, this is a poem of puns and idioms. But I tried to disguise them with enjambment and imagery. I wrote it such that the last image of the line would lead into the next line, but while that new line could connect to the line before, it was also leading into a new image....

Let's take the first stanza. The first image I was hoping to convey was feeling stuck. This starts with the cubical, box, and cardboard. Cubicle and cardboard fit in with a box image, but cardboard also led into the next line with cardboard cut-outs melting in the rain. This next image was of something very tangible disintegrating like dreams halting when you feel lost. The rain leads us to an umbrella which breaks when there is a large gust of wind. And when you are being attacked, you need a shield. So to finish this stanza, I have the feeling of being stuck and feeling like your dreams are fading away and that feels like a hit to the face. The whole stanza drifted between concrete and abstract images so to land the stanza on a concrete image, I have Flat Stanley, a boy who was crushed by a board and became a few inches thick.

The poem ends with the thought that even if my life is crazy good and crazy bad, there is comfort and a Savior that is with me through all of it.

in hindsight by Erika Woo

honestly, I don't feel like "jingle bells"
or "all is well" or "robin lays an egg"
my eyes are dry and foot's asleep
from sitting on my legs

watching binge shows and the harsh-wind snows
keeping me indoors
"oh well" I sigh, my social life dies
extinct like dinosaurs

this year was tough, hard rock rough
hit with ten-ton force
goodbye dear dreams, I want to scream
and now my throat is hoarse

I was lonely this year, full of fear
and in this I wasn't alone
but God is good, more than understood
as this year has shown

coming to the advent, heart sad and bent
Lord, straighten me up to see
that in the stable, hope asleep in the cradle
joy came for you and me

2020

Hands down, I think this is my favorite christmas poem I've written. The rhythm was fun and sing-songy, brought on by the introduction of "jingle bells"; I hope everyone read the poem with that song in mind.

This poem has a few stanzas all focusing on how life in a pandemic is hectic and lonely and joyful all at the same time. It's so counter intuitive, but even in the midst of hardships and suffering, we can have joy and hope. God is unchanging; our light and momentary afflictions are achieving for us an eternal glory that far outweighs them all.

A Starry Perspective – by Erika Woo

I look down from my perch, high above this scene.
I look down and see the census carrying families back to their rusty roots.
Out from new dreamy towns, following old long ruddy roads,
Out from Galilee, two newlyweds, bearing new life,
On the back of a sweating donkey, stop in a stable in Bethlehem.
Alas! Look down the road further and see the shepherds come with their flocks
(all them sheep!)
Down farther to the king sitting plump in a fraying throne
Down past him to the wise men from the East, bringing gifts of laud
Up to the cradle towards the light of the world with love
Love, love, love, love
Shining up at me as I shine the way for others to find
The good news of great joy.[1]

---

[1] I took an entire semester of Whitman :))

2019

Ah, that semester of Whitman was life-changing. For those who know Whitman's work, I'm sure the poem I drew inspiration from was blatant: "Out of the Cradle Endlessly Rocking". And for those who have yet to peruse this great American poet's work, I highly suggest reading a few. "When I heard the Learn'd Astronomer" is my favorite Whitman piece and it's only 8 lines long!

Far from the lights of home,
the familiarity of wet concrete sidewalks
the blessed hands that prepare meals
and smells of overworked ovens
I sit wondering what this Christmas will bring
far away from my parents' home

And I know it's only for a short time
I left home on a mission to study and work
and made a promise that
in the spring I will return again.

Traveling far from the glorious lights above
the warmth of familiar gold streets
and sounds of hallelujah choruses
to a barren evil land far below
did Jesus wonder what Christmas would be
far from his Father's house?

And He knew it was only for a short time
He left home on a mission to do good work
and fulfill a promise knowing that

in the spring he would return home again

- Erika Woo 2018

I got a few messages after this poem went out, asking if I wasn't going home for Christmas. I was. But this idea of connecting the end of Spring semester to Easter was too good to pass up.

There's a story that starts at the beginning
when there was darkness all around
then glorious light was called forth
land took shape and water swirled
creatures crawled and swam
and God held community with humans

Then a different kind of darkness ruled
because of temptation and lust
and the serpent slithered
and man and woman broke the holy tie
cursed to work and toil in pain
brothers fought and towers fell
floods rose and families moved
but all was still not well

Kings came and went
but none brought lasting salvation
as kingdoms were built and destroyed
Prophets spoke of God's great plan
warned of disasters
and brought word of bad news to the lands
Priests sacrificed many a lamb
blood constantly split to forgive the dark
and hope and peace were hard found

Oh sing of a victorious king
who will build a mighty fortress
no more fear no more pain
Oh sing to a wise prophet
who will bring the good news
no more sickness no more death
Oh sing for a holy priest
who will rid this land of plague
no more sacrifice no more blood

And it came to pass
that the spotless lamb
the king, the prophet, the priest
the little baby born in the light of a brilliant star
brought forth a hope and a peace

that forever will keep
he poured his blood
erasing the darkness in hearts
through death
then rose to live with us again
the perfect love story
magnifying his glory
- Erika Woo 2017

Here we have Jesus in three offices: prophet, priest and king. I tried tracing the need for a perfect prophet, an efficient priest and a glorious king throughout history. "What can wash away our sins? Nothing but the blood of Jesus."

I've often found myself skimming over or skipping the genealogies in the Bible. But this year I had been amazed at Matthew 1:1-17 and how Jesus' genealogy traced God's covenant with his people for the promised Messiah.

When In Control

When all else fails you'll see
there are friends who care enough
to be by your side, stay through the fight
Friends who'll help reshape your reality

When all else fails you'll understand
there is family to back you up
Keep you safe, keep you sturdy in place
Loving family close at hand

When all else fails you'll know
there's a God who recognizes
what you're going through, what it'll come to
A righteous God who is in control.

When sin ran rampant He saw
there was need for a Savior
so He sent one, only begotten son
a Savior to cover every flaw

When the world cried for help He understood
there was a way to come down as a King
in a manger, surrounded by strangers
the King of the world ruling for good

When we were still sinners He knew
there was a way to be the Light
to burn bright, shine in the night
a Light of the world through and through.

Erika Woo 2016

I've never been a fan of an ABBA rhyme scheme. In my opinion, they never flow quite as well as ABAB. I tried it out here with the thread of see/saw, understand/understood, know/knew to connect the stanzas.

Take a moment to vent: and lament the ads
That never relent with content that lacks the
Extend of the true meaning of advent where
Forgetting is frequent and we watch sales go
Up by percent while we question the intent
And the lines we'd rather circumvent this
Really is a tiring event because we are all
Stuck in tinsel cement but it's all by our
Consent that we buy into dissent where the
Kings of orient sit in the back of our mind
And ferment only rising the rent in this
Flashy segment a whirling twirling torment
-Repent! And invent a way out of the tent
That leave our view bent making all that we
Spent seem worth more than our discontent
And puts unnecessary accent on a
Supplement to what Jesus underwent go
Represent then maybe we'll make an indent
Or will we all just forget and think that it's
Only about present and not about presence
Just take a moment... and think about what
It all really meant.
By Erika Woo 2015

Around this time I was really into slam poetry; this was my Christmas slam. I recorded myself reciting the poem, put it on youtube, then sent the poem out with the link to the video. I am pretty sure I've since deleted that video, but I am proud of young Erika for the multi-media attempt.

It's easy to forget on Christmas,
That the gifts we get were meant for the King
I admittingly often forget
That the star on top of the tree was
The guide to shepherds and wise men alike.
I always take for granted
All the food i have to eat, when Jesus
Broke bread and shared it with his friends.
And I sometimes don't recall
That the tree strung with ornaments
Once held the crucified Light of the World
When it all comes down to it,
I know I won't remember
What you gave me and what he
Gave her and what i gave you,
But I hope I never forget
What He gave me, on that night
We now call Christmas.

With my feet toasted
And my bread burnt
I rush out the door
Passing lighted trees, wrapped boxes
And overly sparkled windows
On my way to work
I bury my head in paper
And my hand cramps up
People outside the window
Make an awful racket
And when i drive home
All tired and grumpy
I put my hand up to block
The blinding light in the sky
I step inside my house and
The smell of broiled meat
Makes me want to throw up

The kids are shrieking something terrible
And i take an advil to stop the pounding
But as I wrap myself up
In my cozy bed and look at the date
I gasp and bolt up straight.
I missed it.
Merry Christmas
2014

This year I had written two poems this year and couldn't decide which one to send so I put them back to back and sent it out as one poem. I consider this a mistake. Sure, there's the general theme of forgetting and remembering, but the two stanzas are so different in voice and clearly were meant to be two poems. Please read them as if they were two.

A Christmas Song

by Erika

What child is this? Why it's the
sweet little Jesus boy, so
go tell it on the mountain, that
love has come.
You're here now, as
it came upon a midnight clear,
the night that Christ was born, somewhere
away in a manger. Please
come, o come Emmanuel on this
holy night, and
come all ye faithful to the
little town of Bethlehem. Listen!
Do you hear what I hear? If not,
Hark! The herald angels sing
a prayer for every year. So
sing Mary sing, with
the little drummer boy, a
Christmas lullaby to fill this
silent night. Oh
Mary, did you know? This is such
a strange way to save the world, that this
Emmanuel,
the breath of heaven, will bring
joy to the world.
Christmas can't be very far away, because
it's beginning to look a lot like Christmas, so
let it snow so we can have a
white Christmas, even though
all I want for Christmas is
a Christmas to remember so
I'll be home for Christmas to take a
sleigh ride through the glorious
winter wonderland to find the perfect
Christmas tree. Remember,
this Christmas
Rudolph the red nosed reindeer will
deck the halls, look!
here comes Santa Claus

up on the house top.
Christmas time is here, so shout
we wish you a merry Christmas!, because
it's the most wonderful time of the year, whisper
have yourself a merry little Christmas. All this,
til the season comes round again.
2013

This was definitely a fun poem to write, but not so easy to read. As you can see, every line starts with the title of a Christmas song… which means I wrote maybe 5% of this poem.

Christmas Comes

by Erika Woo

Christmas comes with angels dancing
Christmas comes with window glancing
Christmas comes with warm smiles
Christmas comes with snow in piles
Christmas comes with children singing
Christmas comes with sleigh bells ringing
Christmas comes with wrapped presents
Christmas comes with holiday events
Christmas comes with scrumptious food
Christmas comes with everyone in a good mood
Christmas comes with joyful shouts
When Christmas comes there are no doubts
But do you remember the true reason
Of why we celebrate this holiday season
It's not about the boxes with bows
It's about God's Son who chose
To come to this earth as a little boy
So when you unwrap your new toy
Thank God for all that you have
And everything that is to come

2012

By now you might have guessed that anaphoras (the repetition of the beginning of a phrase) are my favorite literary device. You would be correct.

"Ornament"
By Erika Woo

I am a beauty that makes you stop and stare
I am the sphere that is painted with care
I am a ball that put up so everyone can see
I am the decoration that sparkles near the top of the tree

My job is to make you believe that it is true
that Santa is coming with presents for you
and also that Jesus was born on this night
He will always be with you but just out of sight

2011

Writing first person from an inanimate object, classic AABB rhyme scheme, clear rhythm, a whole stanza of anaphora… I'd consider this a classic Erika poem. Let's take it a step further: a poem that starts with the trimmings and trappings of Christmas then brings it back to Jesus? Classic Erika Christmas poem.

2009

Christmas Morning

By: Erika Woo

"Sleigh bells are ringing, and
Alarms are buzzing, and
Children are squealing, and
Friends are hugging, and
Parents are smiling, and
Carolers are singing, and
Stores are closing, and
Stoves are cooking, and
Snow balls are flying, and
You,
you're sleeping in?!?!"

Maybe you've noticed we've skipped 2010. I cannot find it. I looked in my old laptops, all my google drives, and my parent's house basement closets. Perhaps I didn't write one but I'm sure I've just misplaced it. Most of these were hand written on random pieces of paper before being typed up for distribution. If you have my 2010 poem laying around someone, please send it my way.

2009 Erika, you have surprised me with not an anaphora but an epistrophe (the repetition of the end of successive phrases)! Let's ignore the font choice for a minute (or forever,) and applaud the little joke at the end.

Today is Christmas!!
By: Erika Woo

Today is Christmas day
In December not April or May
I wake up Christmas morning as the smell of pancakes fills the air
I hurry with my dressing and the brushing of my tangled hair
For last night I dreamt very peacefully
Of Jesus resting gracefully
And of stockings filled to the very top
Until my eyes opened with a pop
Because in December comes the snow
And it's very cold as you all know
Downstairs I see the beautiful tree
Underneath are presents waiting just for me
But the greatest gift I shall tell you all
No, I shall scream it down the assembly hall!!
Today is the day of Jesus' birth
The day he came down to earth
Today is Christmas so to you I say…
Merry Christmas to all and to all a good day!!
2008

I have a very vivid memory of writing this poem. I had taken a seat at the kitchen table with a stack of printer paper that had pre-printed pink flowers (daisies?) along all four borders. I wrote the poem really quickly but then went back over it with a thesaurus that I had just gotten for my birthday. I forget all the words I switched but I remember switching hall to assembly hall… because my thesaurus had said a synonym for hall was assembly hall. The only thing I would edit are the double exclamation points!!

Christmas poem 2005

☺ HOLIDAY SEASON ☺

Bells are ringing.
Lights are shining.
Kids are dreaming of presents.

In the morning,
Children are playing.
Kids are baking cookies.
What a treat!

Doorbells are ringing.
Doors are opening.
People are walking in with happy smiles ☺
and gifts.

Everyone is sleeping now
It is Christmas Eve.

-Erika Woo

This poem is adorable, and I will give 7 year old Erika all the props for learning the keyboard shortcut for ☺ and incorporating the emoji in a poem.

Poems that were never sent:

How to Make Christmas Spirit

~ Serves the world

INSTRUCTIONS:

Gather the feeling of family mixed with the warmth of friendship
Add a pinch of joy and a sprinkle of peace, all bundled up in a chocolate hug
Stir in the knowledge of the newborn king with the love of the Father.
Dump in a whole lot of thankfulness.
Fold in the smiles and laughter
Don't worry about what it looks like, He is in control
Bake in your heart until accepted
Cool for as long as needed
Frost with snow and place ornaments as desired.
Top with a shining star and serve with love.

This one was very, very cheesy; though I liked the idea of a recipe poem.

I don't believe I could even begin to imagine it
A billion blinding lights filling the black sky
Breathlessly beautiful heavenly beings
To behold such a sight is beyond me
Them belting a song of joy and hope to those below
Blasting the trumpets and blaring the news
To pave a path for the shepherds to the baby boy.

And the truth shaking my body to its bones
that the baby boy would spill his blood
blind to all of my many blemishes,
so that I too may be able sing like an angel being
and my heart to forever bear that beat
of those who sang to the sheep bleating their baas
on that Christmas when the blessing blazed down.

It was quiet, quite quiet
Well, it would be if there weren't
hundreds of dull white sheep surrounding me.
It's hard to think when there is so much noise.
With pointless 'baas' and bleating piercing my ears.
Wait, listen! Do you see that?
Hundreds of blindingly white heavenly beings
all around me, making a new noise.
The hallelujahs filled with hope of a new life
blasting into my ears left me speechless.
And I wondered at the little baby
crying, seemingly helpless, for his mother
noise of the animals dimmed under the tears
making music in my ears.

I love the "Wait, listen! Do you see that?" line.

With the last poem too, you can see there was a time I was deeply interested in the plight of the shepherds... but mostly the sheep. I often ponder how not just the shepherds but also the sheep were the first to hear the good news.

www.ingramcontent.com/pod-product-compliance
Ingram Content Group UK Ltd.
Pitfield, Milton Keynes, MK11 3LW, UK
UKHW020418250726
13967UKWH00007B/2700

9 781387 457311